The
LITTLE
BOOK
of
OTTER
PHILOSOPHY

The

LITTLE
BOOK

of

OTTER
PHILOSOPHY

How to Live Life
Like You Otter

Jennifer McCartney

HarperCollins*Publishers*

'It is a happy talent to know how to play.'

Ralph Waldo Emerson

Contents

'Please join me in my quest to be a better otter.
Right after we have a nap. And a snack.
And a swim.'

Part One
An Otter Education

Introduction: Welcome to the Otter Philosophy

S tressed? Overworked? No time for play? There must be an otter way!

Otters are some of the most delightful animals on the planet. These long, lean, furry creatures embody pure joy in so many ways. What other species builds water slides for fun? Or holds hands with their friends just because? Or wraps themselves in seaweed, so they can nap without floating away? These intelligent, water-dwelling mammals are not only an essential part of the world's (and YouTube's) ecosystem, they also have a lot to teach us about the way we live.

In a world obsessed with work and productivity, otters are a reminder about the importance of play.*

---

* Remember when everyone lost their minds over adult colouring books? We're desperate for fun.

They're fun, lively animals that love a good laugh with friends. They don't give a shit about deadlines, or who ate the last bonbon or how many emails are in their inbox. Hell, they don't really stress about anything. 'Just play. Have fun. Enjoy the game' is their motto (and Michael Jordan's). They resist the assumption that being an adult requires a serious, no-nonsense attitude. They embrace playtime like it's their job. They laugh and chatter and take group naps together, to-do lists be damned. And they've also been on this planet in some form or another for around 6 million years – a testament to the value of their way of life, surely? In a world that often feels isolating and lonely, where hard work and productivity are valued above all else, it's high time we recognised the wisdom of these joyful, friendly animals.

If you've been paying attention to the internet or been to the zoo in recent years, you're likely a bit envious of the otter already. We've all seen videos of otters holding hands, playing with balls and nibbling sea urchins (and I mean literally everyone has seen them – these videos have 40 billion views). And everyone from your mum to your best friend sends you otter GIFs, otter birthday cards and links to articles about otters doing cute things. *'Look!'* we seem to be saying, *'Look at this joy! Share this joy with me!'* But perhaps we're also wondering: is this kind of joy really possible? Well, the otter philosophy is here to tell you that it is. And the PLAY method will show you how. So, what's their secret? Why are they so happy? What can we learn from these slippery little joy weasels? Read on, and wonder no more.

The Little Book of Otter Philosophy is packed with otter science, studies on friendship (friends can help you live longer), napping and playfulness (play can keep you feeling younger), quotes, original poems and quizzes to help you live life like you otter.* With chapters on love and friendship, food and drink, leisure and pleasure, work and school, home and the environment and health and happiness, it'll show you how best to incorporate the otter philosophy into every aspect of your life. Plus, the PLAY philosophy will offer a quick and easy way to remember what you've learned. So get ready to reclaim your joy and

---

*   Numerous otter puns are also included for your enjoyment.

have a bit of otterly good fun. More fun than a barrel of monkeys, in fact.*

---

* Otters out-fun monkeys by any measure. Sorry, Curious George.

Let's turn all our assumptions about productivity and our place in a capitalist system upside down!

Follow the PLAY Method
for a More Joyful Life

*'Work consists of whatever a body is obliged
to do. Play consists of whatever a body is
not obliged to do.'*

Mark Twain

Otters love to learn. They're almost insatiably curious about everything and anything. So the first step to following the otter philosophy is learning its key tenets, albeit in an easy, fun way. Now, every book that purports to be helpful requires a neat acronym to help the memory-challenged among us to retain a useful takeaway. So please find here the PLAY method:

P

Plunge in. This probably sounds a bit weird and that's because there aren't a lot of motivational things that begin with 'P'. But the point here is to embrace the elements. Forget about constantly protecting yourself, and be sure to enjoy the opportunity to get wet when it arises – as an otter would. In a literal sense, this means always bringing your swimsuit if there's a pool, lake, hot tub or lazy river at your destination. It means never bringing an umbrella. (If there's wind, it's pointless, and if there's a light drizzle, enjoy the feeling of getting wet.) In a monsoon, you're probably indoors anyway. In a figurative sense, taking the plunge means acting impulsively. Trying new things. Fully committing to your actions. Going all in – no half measures here. You get the idea. Basically, always say yes to skinny dipping. I realise it may seem like people only go skinny dipping in the movies, but if you're young or old or somewhere in between, and someone somewhere asks you if you want to jump naked into a body of water, flabby bits and all, you won't regret saying yes.

L

Laugh about it. Otters technically don't smile or laugh, probably, but they're happy and playful and look to be enjoying life most of the time. Being able to see the funny side of things is an important coping mechanism. The ability to laugh in the midst of our darkest moments is a healthy way of dealing with life's hard knocks. When my dad falls down in public (he has Parkinson's disease), he often jokes that he does it for the attention (specifically, the attention of the ladies who rush to help him up). In fact, black humour is one of the best ways to deal with horrible things, if you can manage it. And it's a great way to deal with the random stupidity that is daily life. Of course, when something's actually funny, it's the best thing in the world to laugh out loud. Not a keyboard LOL, but a true vocal cackle or bark or shriek or guffaw – whatever noise you emit when you're truly happy. And what's so serious, anyway? I mean, I know lots of things are, and it's not about trivialising what's truly important to us. But we'll all be dead soon. Might as well have a bit of fun along the way.

A

Ask why. This step is all about cultivating curiosity.

Curiosity means we are engaged with the world and ensures our brains are always learning new things, which, in turn, keeps us young. You know how when you're around kids they'll ask you things like, 'What is yellow made of?' and, 'What's your favourite kind of bird?' Watch otters at play and you'll notice the same kind of curiosity. They're interested in different rocks, passing fish, toy balls and each other – everything in their line of sight is worthy of investigation. This is the kind of curiosity we should all strive for. Why are things the way they are? What do you think about that thing? What does that other person think about that thing? A good way to practise is to be curious about small things on a day-to-day level and then look up the answer. Any thought you may have about an actor or a book or a date in history or electricity – look it up. You pass by a weird castle or unusual tower on the train? Look it up. Be involved.*

Y

YOLO (also an acronym, I realise). This stands for 'you only live once'. This is true, as far as we know. Unless we're all in the matrix, living simulated digital lives – which is a possibility – we get one shot at life. Whatever it throws at us, that's it. So make sure that whatever you're doing, it's something worthwhile, and that you enjoy it. For stressed-out parents, take heart that raising kids is something that *will be reward-*

---

* Unless you're very drunk and you spot a murder in progress from the train window. Best to just leave that alone.

ing in the future (most likely when the kids have gone to school and start to send you nice texts about how they miss you). It's not about being selfish and doing whatever we feel like. We all still have social obligations and we're all required to be good citizens and participate in society. But it does mean having a bit of perspective. What is it that you're afraid to do? And what's the worst that can happen? Start your podcast. Love your face. Ditch the toxic people. Get a dog. And eat the ice lolly. Preferably while laughing naked in a swimming pool – plunging in being one of the four tenets of the PLAY method after all. Is there one single ice-lolly stick manufacturer, do you think? Or is it a network of individually owned lumber corporations and wood factories that distribute sticks in each country?*

---

* Ice lollies were invented by accident, apparently, when 11-year-old Frank Epperson left his drink and stir stick on his porch overnight, back in 1905; in the morning, he had a frozen treat with a built-in handle. 'Frozen ice on a stick' was born. And this is what curiosity gets you: fun facts to discuss at your next cocktail party ...

Now that you've been introduced to the PLAY method, get ready to learn some amazing otter facts and immerse yourself in the revolutionary otter philosophy. Let's all hold hands and plunge in together, shall we?

My stomach fur is your playground.
Delight in its offerings.

Quiz

What Kind of Otter Are You?

When it comes to gadgets, tools, electronics, you're like:

A. you have the latest model of everything – electric toothbrush, electric car and AI chip in your wrist

B. you own a set of cutlery and a television

C. you pay people to put stuff together for you – no tools needed, ever; wait, you do own a screwdriver. And you use the bottom of your shoe as a hammer.

What best describes your vacation routine?

A. Up at 6 am, checking work email.

B. Piña colada by the pool. Check your work email a bit later when you're drunk.

C. Your life is a non-stop vacation. That's what you like to call unemployment.

When it comes to playtime you prefer:

A. jumping out of aeroplanes with a parachute or off a cliff with a bungee cord

B. adult colouring books – do they count as play? Your therapist recommended them …

C. a game you can play on your phone while lying down.

Answers

Mostly As: otter to the max. You're a very high-octane otter bordering on becoming a hummingbird. Don't forget that life doesn't have to be scheduled or even death-defying. Playing a board game can be just as rewarding as free soloing up a cliff face. So take a page from the otter playbook, and chill.

Mostly Bs: livin' life like you otter. You're dedicated to work, play and whatever you set your mind to, but you're also aware we're all going to die soon, and nothing is that important. A nice, balanced attitude towards being alive.

Mostly Cs: stoned otter. You're so laid-back you're almost a sloth. But you've also got some great otter characteristics – ingenuity, a love of taking it easy and a sense of humour. Keep up the good work, but don't forget otters sometimes have to work hard to play hard.

A raft of otters at rest in the river. Otters also
love a good tongue twister.

Part Two
A Practical Guide

Love and Friendship

'The holy passion of Friendship is so sweet and
steady and loyal and enduring a nature that it
will last through a whole lifetime, if not
asked to lend money.'

Mark Twain

'Love is the only force capable of transforming
an enemy into a friend.'

Martin Luther King, Jr

Otter Fact: Otters like to strike up friendships with other species. These unlikely alliances include cats, goats, dogs and, in some cases, people. One otter in Finland has been visiting his human friend for food and companionship since 2011. Another, named Pip, likes to play tag with his owner's pet cat, Sam.

In a world that can often seem politically divided, lonely and just plain cruel, the otter is a reminder that it's possible (and beneficial) to have friendships with people who are different from ourselves. It can be tough sometimes, though – a 2016 study in the *Journal of Personality and Social Psychology* found that we're hard-wired to choose like-minded friends and partners. We prefer having a comfortable social circle where everyone can relax and take it easy. This is great – until it isn't. Researchers warn that this quest for similarity can result in a lack of exposure to new ideas and perspectives: 'If you hang out only with people who are loony like you, you can be out of touch with the big, beautiful diverse world,' says Chris Crandall,

Otter and kitten enjoy rubber balls, mackerel snacks, and afternoon snuggles. They also like to pose awkwardly for photos.

professor of psychology at Kansas University. So, get out of your comfort zone in order to broaden your worldview. Challenge yourself to chat with people a bit different from yourself. Do they speak another language? Are they very into fitness or meat pies or Brexit? Who knows, it may be the start of a beautiful friendship.

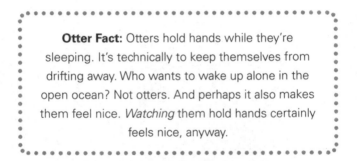

Otter Fact: Otters hold hands while they're sleeping. It's technically to keep themselves from drifting away. Who wants to wake up alone in the open ocean? Not otters. And perhaps it also makes them feel nice. *Watching* them hold hands certainly feels nice, anyway.

Giving and receiving little forms of physical affection is one of a relationship's great joys. Whether it's entangled legs on a couch with your best friend, or a rub of the shoulders on a crowded train from a partner, or a deep, loving hug from a parent or grandparent, these expressions of affection are what make life worth-

Otters prefer snuggles to handshakes.

while. And they keep us healthier, too. According to Professor Tiffany Field, director of the Touch Research Institute at the University of Miami School of Medicine, touch 'leads to a chain of bioelectric and chemical changes that basically relax the nervous system'. That means a simple touch actually releases the feel-good hormone oxytocin and lowers levels of the primary stress hormone, cortisol. So something as simple as holding hands can lower blood pressure, reduce stress and calm the heart rate. The effects are lasting, too. Studies show the mental benefits of physical affection last until the following day: a hug today can put us in a better mood tomorrow. So, make like an otter and show someone how much you care. A furry friend. A bestie. A mum or dad. A stuffed animal. Whatever! Give someone you love a hug.*

---

* Do not hug strangers, co-workers or generally touch anyone without their consent. Do not be a creep.

'I was in the Virgin Islands once. I met a girl. We ate lobster, drank piña coladas. At sunset, we made love like sea otters. That was a pretty good day. Why couldn't I get that day over and over and over?'

Bill Murray

Otter Fact: Otters are an extremely chatty bunch. They have nine distinct vocalisations they use to communicate – they are: whistles, chirps, chuckles, clicks, coos, whines, snarls, screams and growls.

It should be evident that communication is the key to any successful relationship. Luckily, we have the ability to communicate with our loved ones instantaneously, 24 hours a day, via texting, video chats, email and direct messaging. There's also old-fashioned phone calls and, of course, we even see each other in person occasionally, too. So why does it feel so tough, sometimes? Why do we feel distant from our loved

'I meant what I said when I texted you that GIF.'

ones, or misunderstood, ignored or unfulfilled? Just like everything else in life, good communication takes practice.

According to Dr Michelle Rosser-Majors, a professor of psychology at Ashford University: 'As human beings, we aspire to feel competent, valued and appreciated. Positive words have this type of power, creating the solid foundations needed to build strong, productive relationships that resonate clear lines of communications.' So – this may sound blindingly obvious, but part of successful communication is saying nice things to people you care about once in a while. One way to do this is to use 'words of affirmation', according to Gary Chapman, author of *The Five Love Languages: How to Express Heartfelt Commitment to Your Mate*. This means offering kind, encouraging words as often as possible – including unsolicited compliments, expressions of gratitude or words of endearment. And this isn't just a bit of feel-good advice, either. It's scientifically proven to make both parties feel better.

In the book *Words Can Change Your Brain* by Andrew Newberg and Mark Robert Waldman, the

'Let's playfully communicate our way into a
successful long-term relationship.'

authors found that both speaking and hearing positive words could increase cognitive reasoning, strengthen our frontal lobes and motivate us to repeat the behaviour that inspired the affirmative words. So next time you're feeling praise-y, don't forget to let your friend or partner know. *That cup of tea you made was so great! I had so much fun on the water slide today! I appreciate the advice you gave me about how I need to pluck my chin hairs once in a while!* You know, nice things like that. And if you're texting, don't forget the exclamation mark. In a study in 2016, psychologist Danielle Gunraj found that texts punctuated with a full stop were perceived as being insincere. And, conversely, linguists have found that multiple exclamation marks convey honesty.

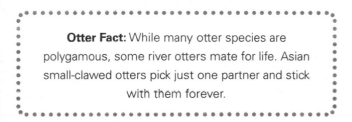

Otter Fact: While many otter species are polygamous, some river otters mate for life. Asian small-clawed otters pick just one partner and stick with them forever.

How do otters make a long-term relationship work? We can't ask them directly, but it's safe to assume it involves a lot of fun and games. According to psychiatrist Dr Stuart Brown, head of the National Institute for Play, a light-hearted approach to intimacy can help a partnership stay healthy. 'The couples who sustain a sense of mutual playfulness with each other tend to work out the wrinkles in their relationships much better than those who are really serious,' he says in an interview with NPR in the States. And a sense of humour is important, too. According to research done by human development and family studies professor Brian Ogolsky at the University of Illinois Urbana-Champaign, couples who use humour to defuse situations are more likely to stay together than those who don't. It isn't about being funny, though, he notes. It's about how we use humour in times of stress – turning a potentially negative interaction into a positive one.

Finally, what seems to be obvious is supported by science: doing fun activities with a loved one can be beneficial to the relationship. A study entitled 'Compatibility, Leisure and Satisfaction in Marital

Relationships' found that a relationship benefited from shared leisure time *as long as both partners enjoyed the activity*. (That means if one person isn't into it,★ the whole relationship actually suffers.) So find your compatible interests, and make time for them: suntanning, hitting up the art gallery, playing darts, going to the movies, saving the elephants,† whatever you want, as long as you both enjoy it.

> *'In the sweetness of friendship let there be laughter, and sharing of pleasures. For in the dew of little things the heart finds its morning and is refreshed.'*
>
> *Khalil Gibran*

Otter Fact: Otters wrap themselves in kelp to help anchor themselves while they nap.

★   Likely golf. Sorry, Grandad, it's just so boring.
†   Harry and Meghan are going to be just fine.

Way more fun than being tangled in bedsheets.*

*Tangled in kelp, that is. Not unspooled
cassette tape.

We once saw a bunch of very sunburned people floating in inner tubes down the Bow River which runs through downtown Calgary, Canada. There were about 20 in the group, each one's tube linked to the next, and all holding a can of Budweiser, except for the few who appeared to be napping. Styrofoam containers with more beer floated behind them, also tethered by ropes. Bathrooms? Not important. Mobiles? Nope. Sunblock? Didn't look like it. All we heard was laughter, conversation and the pleasant hum of the river as it washed them downstream – a magic web of drunk friendship. This kind of dedication to both nap and playtime, drinking and friendship, is definitely something to strive for. How can you up your nap game? A weighted blanket? A drop of melatonin? A hammock? A body pillow? What about your friendships? Time for a bit of axe-throwing? Canoeing? A simple pub crawl? Whatever you decide, I wish for you the kind of joy that comes from being drunk in a river in an inner-tube convoy with your best mates. That's the stuff friendships are made of.

'True friends stab you in the front.'

Oscar Wilde

Otter Fact: Otters might look soft and cuddly, but they remain dangerous wild animals. They bite. They sometimes practise necrophilia.* The males of the species often bite and drown their partners.

We love to love otters. They're sweet and joyful and fun to watch. And yet … (see above). Basically, this is a good reminder that sometimes the things we love can disappoint, surprise and even hurt us. This is a huge bummer, but it's just a fact of being alive and a consequence of having relationships with other living things. People aren't perfect. They have issues. They do things we don't approve of, or we can't forgive. They're kind of jerks, sometimes. And more often than not, they don't change. The otter philosophy is

* Yikes.

about recognising that, and figuring out what we're ok with. This isn't about forgiving the unforgivable or excusing abusive behaviour. But it's about acknowledging that people can and will surprise us in all kinds of ways, both good and bad, and that's part of life. It's how we were designed. So if you're the one that's let someone down, don't be too hard on yourself – or on them, if it's the other way around. Apologise or forgive (or don't and move on to a hopefully healthier situation), but take heart that even the best, most adorable things in nature are also complete assholes sometimes.

Otter Mythology Around the World

Otters feature in folklore from communities across the globe. From Iceland to Iraq to indigenous nations on the West Coast of North America, otters are revered for their mischievous, playful ways and their ability to shapeshift.

- Keoonik (pronounced cue-nick) is the star of a few Mi'kmaq folktales. True to otter form, he spends most of his time fooling around, causing trouble and playing jokes on his fellow animals. He's never malevolent, though. That's not the otter way.

- In Zoroastrian culture, whose people reside mainly in Iran and India, otters are considered sacred. In fact, they are called water-dogs and are believed to be the reincarnation of many individual dogs. Basically, a single otter is millions of wonderful doggies all smushed into one new being – who is presumably a *very* good boy.

- In Norse mythology, *Otter's Ransom* is a tale about a group of three gods who kill an otter for its pelt, only to discover it is a man who takes the shape of an otter by day. When the man's family discover the murder, they demand from the hunter gods a ransom of gold to atone for their crime.

- In Japan's Ishikawa Prefecture, stories are told of otters who shapeshift into beautiful young women. These otter-women speak cryptic words and play pranks, like fooling passers-by into sumo wrestling with rocks and tree stumps. Occasionally, they also kill and eat men who approach them. That one took a dark turn, eh?

It's hard to be crabby when life is so delicious.

Food and Drink

'All you need is love. But a little chocolate now and then doesn't hurt.'

Charles M. Schulz

'You don't need a silver fork to eat good food.'

Paul Prudhomme

Otter Fact: Otters like to eat food off their tummies while floating on their backs.

Ronald Reagan once said that 'you can tell a lot about a fellow's character by his way of eating jellybeans', which is just the sort of judgmental nonsense the otter philosophy seeks to avoid. The otter prefers to be comfortable, the better to enjoy its snacks. Who among us hasn't rested a tub of ice cream on ourselves while wrapped snugly in a blanket watching our favourite show? Or wedged a snack or drink in between our knees for easy access while driving? The otter philosophy is about letting go of the 'shoulds' that society serves us and making do with what we have. We all gotta eat. And it's nice to let go of the judgments of how exactly we should be eating, sometimes. 'Oh, you prefer a properly set dinner table with cloth napkins, your Majesty? You're such a badger!'* Just the kind of attitude we don't endorse.

Bertha Naps and Carries On

There once was an otter named Bertha,
Who ate fish to the point of inertia.
Her stomach got bloated –
To recover, she floated,
Then resolved to have some desert-a.

---

* Badgers think they're so fancy.

> **Otter Fact:** Otters mostly eat stuff they find in the water, like crayfish, frogs and crabs. But sometimes, to keep things interesting, they eat rabbits. Or rats. And even a bird or two.

The otter philosophy is all about embracing new things, and that includes stuff we eat. So, if you're at an event and someone offers you a deep-fried scorpion on a cracker, eat it. Say yes to everything. The world is wide and wonderful, and you never know what's out there waiting for you, if only you're open to it. In Iceland, you might be offered minke whale steak or fermented shark; in Iqaluit or Toronto, seal tartare; in some parts of the UK, deep-fried chocolate bars; or in Turkey, the best baklava in the world. Wherever you are, be sure to enjoy the local cuisine. But you don't necessarily have to travel far to enjoy new things. New restaurant in town? Check it out. Goat-flavoured jerky at the petrol station? Buy it and eat it. Spray cheese in a can?* Put it

---

* Welcome to the USA.

'That's 41 somersaults in a row, Larry.
Can we get lunch now?'

in your mouth. New experiences are key to keeping you young, playful, joyful and open.

Unfortunate Fred

There once was a sea urchin, Fred,
Who was contentedly snuggled in bed,
When along came an otter,
Hunting deep in the water,
Now Fred's been digested instead.

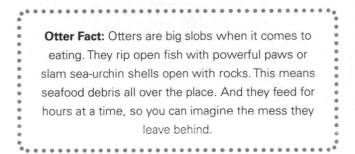

Otter Fact: Otters are big slobs when it comes to eating. They rip open fish with powerful paws or slam sea-urchin shells open with rocks. This means seafood debris all over the place. And they feed for hours at a time, so you can imagine the mess they leave behind.

The otter philosophy encourages eating with wild abandon, the way nature intended. And we can learn a lot from the blissfully untidy otter when it comes to our own dining habits – because, according to science,

**Enjoying a pint of Ben & Jerry's 'Phish Food',
probably.**

allowing mealtimes to be a bit joyful and a bit messy helps us to develop a healthy attitude towards food. For example, researchers at De Montfort University in Leicester asked kids to search for toys buried in mashed potatoes and jelly, and found that those kids who were eager to play with their food were less likely to be fussy eaters.* And some restaurant critics take great pride in their ability to destroy shirt, table-cloth, tie or lipstick with a big, messy meal. To these lovers of food, a table's lack of cleanliness is in direct proportion to how much they have enjoyed them-selves. There's no time for tiny bites, carefully speared morsels and delicate dabbing with napkins when a delicious dish appears before them. A good way to practise this skill is to order or cook something that's notoriously messy. A big bucket of crab legs. A giant bowl of ramen. Chicken wings. Corn on the cob. A burrito. And plunge in. Feel the grease and sauce and butter and broth on your face, watch them gloop all

---

*   Some poor kids in this study refused to get their hands dirty. Presumably they're all accountants or professional wardrobe organisers now.

over the table, your shirt, your hands. And resist the urge for a napkin. Mealtime is sometimes a bit of a mess, and there's a lot of joy to be had from embracing that.

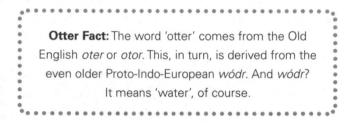

Otter Fact: The word 'otter' comes from the Old English *oter* or *otor*. This, in turn, is derived from the even older Proto-Indo-European *wódr*. And *wódr*? It means 'water', of course.

Water is what makes an otter an otter. An otter lives in water and naps in water and generally relies on water for just about everything. Water is the key to all life, in fact. It's in our cells and bones and brains. It's sloshing around in there, nourishing all our little inner spaces, as we go about our business. It's good for us. We know this. It comprises up to 60 per cent of our bodies, so it must be important. But there's lots of finger-wagging these days about how we're not drinking enough of it. There are online calculators showing how many glasses a day a person needs to drink based on body weight, and articles about how even the *sensation* of thirst means you're already dehydrated. It can feel a bit discouraging to hear that in order to be healthy, *all* a person needs is eight glasses a day. Especially when all you drank yesterday was coffee, four glasses of wine and some fizzy water with your ibuprofen tablet. But the otter philosophy is, of course, without judgment. All it asks is that you think about water once in a while. Swim in it. Bathe in it. Give thanks for it. For all its wonderful lubricating and hydrating and regulating and cushioning and cleansing abilities. And drink it occasionally, when you remember. Right now is probably as good a time as any.

A Classic Otter Cocktail

Otters don't have expensive tastes when it comes to booze. They're more interested in socialising with friends than worrying about what's in their glass. In fact, they're open to drinking just about anything at all. With that in mind, I give you the otter's favourite cocktail: the Sea Breeze. Simple, refreshing and best enjoyed with an ocean view and, ideally, some wildlife – if you're lucky.

Ingredients
120ml (4fl oz) vodka
60ml (2fl oz) cranberry juice
30ml (1fl oz) grapefruit juice
a lime wedge

Method
Combine the vodka with the cranberry and grape-fruit juices and serve over ice with a lime wedge.

Leisure and Pleasure

'We don't stop playing because we grow old; we grow old because we stop playing.'

George Bernard Shaw

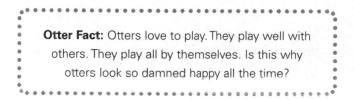

Otter Fact: Otters love to play. They play well with others. They play all by themselves. Is this why otters look so damned happy all the time?

The otter philosophy is all about acknowledging the benefits of play and making time for it in our daily lives. For adults, play can be a therapeutic way to reduce stress and increase a sense of wellbeing. A 2013 study in the *European Journal of Humour Research* (yes,

'Thanks to these fun rocks, I no longer feel the crushing weight of the world on my shoulders.'

this is a real thing) found that the more playful a person was, the more likely they were to report a high level of life satisfaction. Another 2013 study, in the journal *Leisure Sciences*, found that playful people reported lower stress levels and were 'less likely to employ negative, avoidant and escape-oriented strategies'. And according to Dr Stuart Brown, founder of the National Institute for Play (yes, this also exists), there are consequences for those of us who take life too seriously: 'What you begin to see when there's major play deprivation in an otherwise competent adult is that they're not much fun to be around,' he warns in an interview with NPR in the US. 'You begin to see that the perseverance and joy in work are lessened and that life is much more laborious.' Sound like anyone you know?

What constitutes 'play' is different for each individual, but generally, if it feels like work, it isn't play. And if you're focused on the outcome, it isn't play. Play is doing something for the sake of doing it, results be damned! That can include anything from collecting stamps or reading a book to playing football or climbing Mount Everest. So next time you're stressed and find yourself reaching for a giant bottle of Buckfast or the TV remote (escape-oriented strategies), perhaps consider jumping in a puddle instead. Or playing a game on your phone. Or climbing a mountain. The long-term benefits are worth it.

> *'I was wise enough to never grow up
> while fooling most people into
> believing I had.'*
>
> *Margaret Mead*

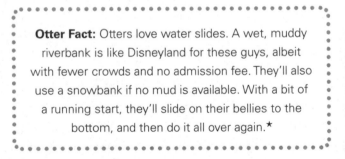

Otter Fact: Otters love water slides. A wet, muddy riverbank is like Disneyland for these guys, albeit with fewer crowds and no admission fee. They'll also use a snowbank if no mud is available. With a bit of a running start, they'll slide on their bellies to the bottom, and then do it all over again.★

★ Some joyless researchers have suggested that otters use water slides as a form of easy travel, and not play. But come on.

The Otter National Holiday

Otters love mischief, so it follows that April Fools' Day is near-sacred within the species. What better way to celebrate the silly, ephemeral nature of life than with a harmless, hopefully non-irritating prank among friends? Admittedly, these days, the holiday has become a bit tiresome, with every corporate brand getting in the act with jokey social-media campaigns. Even back in 1957, for example, the BBC broadcast a *faux* documentary purporting to show something called the Swiss Spaghetti Harvest. So many rubes apparently called in asking where they could get one of these spaghetti plants, the hosts had to fess up it was fake. Luckily, there are lots of pure, joyful ways to enjoy this holiday with friends while not seeming like a twat. Here are some otter-approved pranks for work or home:

Otter-approved Nonsense

- Completely papering over work items like computers or chairs in multicoloured sticky notes is a colourful way to let your colleagues know you love them. Also, it looks very pretty and makes for great photos.

- Tape a little headshot of your friend's fave celebrity over the peephole of their door. Give a knock and allow them to delightedly open their home to Nicholas Cage, Carla Bruni or Margaret Thatcher.* Actually, taping photos of celebrities (or cats) to random things is a great year-round endeavour.

- Rearrange the keys on a colleague's computer. This little gag vows QWERTY no more! Switch things around with a neat little message like HI JAN or just aim for a bit of arbitrary nonsense.

- Anything with balloons.

* The first time these three have appeared in a sentence together.

Sliding into Mondays like wheeee! Mainly
because otters don't have jobs.

The otter philosophy is all about finding your water slide. This isn't meant to be one of those hokey inspirational mantras encouraging you to 'find your bliss' in an eco-treehouse. It isn't about buying expensive adult toys★ or heading anywhere fancy. After all, when we were children, playtime didn't always mean sitting down in a sandbox with a bunch of toys – it meant blowing bubbles in our milk, doing a cartwheel, capturing crickets in glass jars (if we were some kind of sociopath) and finding shapes in clouds (the sky where I grew up had a lot of wizards). It's about recognising opportunities for fun in our daily lives and embracing them – right then and there. Swings at the nearby park? Swing. Leaf pile? Kick. Crossword puzzle in the waiting room? Eight across is probably 'oboe'. Novelty tiki mugs or T-shirts for sale at the cocktail bar? You get the idea. Look at the world as your childhood self would. Or as an otter would. With an eye for fun. Immediate rewards. A bit of a laugh. And embrace the water slides available to you every day.

★   Golf clubs, go-karts, fancy hairdryers.

'The creation of something new is not accomplished by the intellect but by the play instinct.'

Carl Jung

Otter Fact: Wet riverbanks are made of mud. Which means otters get very dirty come playtime.

When's the last time you got really dirty? For me it was when a university friend asked if I wanted to go mud sliding during a thunderstorm. This was after a few tequila shots, so all of us in attendance said yes. And out we ran, in our oldest sweatpants and T-shirts, into the rain. We slid around, slapped mud on one another and generally acted a bit stupid and carefree. Outside, away from air-conditioning and sanitised flooring and in an environment filled with mud and drunk friendship, we embraced a bit of nature. We were covered in it. And, according to science, we were a little less likely to get sick as a result.

'The boots are coming off right after this photo shoot.'

Microbes, like those found in dirt, stimulate our immune response and keep us healthy, according to Professor Jack Gilbert, director of the Microbiome Center at the University of Chicago and co-author of *Dirt is Good: The Advantage of Germs for Your Child's Developing Immune System*. For example, a 2016 study in the *Journal of Allergy and Clinical Immunology* found that Amish children, who live on small farms, are less likely to suffer allergies and asthma than kids raised in the city. Another study, published in the journal *Pediatrics*, found that the children of parents who 'cleaned' their dropped dummies by licking them were less liable to suffer from asthma, allergies and eczema than those whose dummies were sterilised. The theory is that children on farms and those who are given not-so-clean pacifiers are exposed to more dirt – and the healthy microbes that dirt contains. This exposure causes their immune systems to adapt, evolve and get stronger. The lesson here is simple: get dirty once in a while. Lick something weird. Not only is it fun, it's good for you. As Professor Gilbert says, 'Rescue a dog, let them eat food off the floor, play in the soil. Dirt is good!'

'It's better to play than do nothing.'

Confucius

Otter Fact: Otters feature in some of the world's best-loved literature. People just love reading about otters, as the book you're holding proves.

The Wind in the Willows by Kenneth Grahame stars lovable Otter and his son Portly. Otter is a well-mannered creature who despises material wealth and excessive noise. Classic otter.

Ted Hughes wrote a poem called 'An Otter'. In it, he compares the otter to things like kings, eels and tomcats. At the end of the poem the otter is reduced to a pelt slung over the back of a chair, which is a bummer. But that's the way it goes sometimes.

Tarka the Otter: His Joyful Water-Life and Death in the Country of the Two Rivers is a novel by Henry Williamson which was published in 1927. Today's savvy editors probably wouldn't stand for such a long subtitle, but never mind. It follows the life and times of Tarka the otter around rural England. The author turned out to be a big fan of fascism, so his works aren't so popular now.

In *Ring of Bright Water*, Gavin Maxwell writes about his life on the west coast of Scotland in a cottage with his pet otter, Mijbil. An otter that he brought back from Iraq, for some reason. The book has it all – otter high jinks, a fast friendship, 'an otter fixation' and, of course, murder and heartbreak. It's billed by many critics as one of the most popular nature books ever written.

And finally, in J. K. Rowling's *Harry Potter and the Order of the Phoenix* we discover that Hermione Granger's patronus is an otter. A fitting animal companion for the intelligent, sassy and mischievous Granger. In fact, Rowling has said that the otter is her favourite animal. Her ideal job, the author revealed to her followers in 2014 (besides being an author), was 'otter weigher'.

'We all need empty hours in our lives or we will have no time to create or dream.'

Robert Coles, American child psychologist

Otter Fact: Otters spend a few hours a day at play. How many? It's not an exact science: they tend to goof off a bit more once their immediate needs are met, and a bit less when food is scarce or the females are nursing.

Imagine that. In a world where everything is measured by money and productivity, imagine if we set aside time and energy for … play. The same way we set aside time for meditation, or homework or social media – a little slice of the day just for us. The benefits would be pretty amazing: increased levels of happiness and creativity.

So how much playtime would be beneficial to *your* overall wellbeing? Well, the otter philosophy isn't about exact measurements and planning ahead, but

'Do you have any shellfish?'
'Go fish.'
'With pleasure.'

two and a half hours daily seems like a good number to aim for. A 2019 paper entitled 'The Effects of Being Time Poor and Time Rich on Life Satisfaction' found that for those who were employed, two and a half hours of free time corresponded to the highest amount of reported happiness. Those who didn't work were happiest with just under five hours of free time.* Finding these spare hours during the day may seem like an impossible goal, but playtime could help make you happier and more satisfied. So, write a letter, buy a set of colourful markers, take a walk in the park, hit up a bookstore, water your plants – or maybe this is a great opportunity to paint a picture or write a book. According to the findings of a 2012 study published in *Psychological Science*, 'Inspired by Distraction: Mind Wandering Facilitates Creative Incubation', free time can actually help make us more creative. When the mind is allowed to wander, to

---

* Otters don't wear pyjamas, but rest assured that they are an otter-approved human garment, especially if you're unemployed or taking a day off. Nakedness is preferred, of course.

daydream, to free-associate, interesting and unusual connections can result. Bam. You're an artist now. Congrats.

> *'Be patient and calm. No one can catch fish in anger.'*
>
> *Herbert Hoover*

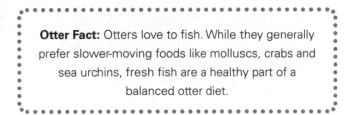

Otter Fact: Otters love to fish. While they generally prefer slower-moving foods like molluscs, crabs and sea urchins, fresh fish are a healthy part of a balanced otter diet.

If you have ever been fishing, you'll know what a unique, relaxing activity it can be. It's contemplative, slow and largely unnecessary (if you live near a supermarket). Meditative pastimes, like fishing, are classic examples of adult 'play'. It isn't quite child's play, but it's definitely not work. In fact, as long as you're kind of enjoying yourself, even things like folding laundry

Have you ever seen a more adorable drawing
of a bird? Just look at it. Life is
wonderful sometimes.

can offer a bit of respite from the daily grind. Hiking, knitting, dancing, pottery, woodworking – all of these activities fall into this middle ground between play and work. And in a world packed with deadly serious things,* these otter-approved, not-*quite*-pointless activities can be an easy way to embrace the otter philosophy when you just don't have time for joyful play. The act of fishing, for example, is beneficial to the fisherperson in a number of ways: it offers time spent outdoors in nature, physical activity, increased exposure to vitamin D and mental and emotional downtime. In fact, a Finnish study from 2009 found that men who fished had a 22 per cent lower mortality rate than those who didn't. The study found something else surprising: the *partners* of those who went fishing enjoyed a *35 per cent* lower mortality rate than the partners of those who didn't. So while these meditative types of activities can be good for your own health, it's worth noting they are also beneficial to the ones you love.

---

* Utility bills, for example. Or movie spoilers.

An Ode to Play

When you're feeling like you otter
Be a better son or daughter
Or mum or wife or man or beast
And bake your bread with a bit more yeast …
And do your homework!
Or start to try!
Or get things done!
And by and by …
The stress feels near,
You're overwhelmed.
Too much to do
With this and that. The other, too.

Then *rise*, dear one, and face the day,
Resolve to spend it all at play:

A lazy stretch
A dawdle, too
A whack-a-ball
A nothing at all
Some colouring books
A fort in a nook

Some bubbly booze
A post-play snooze

'Cause what's a life without some fun?
The thing, that's best, when day is done.

> **Otter Fact:** A group of otters on land is called a romp (in water it's called a raft). A romp is an appropriate collective noun if you've ever seen a bunch of otters hanging out. Are they sitting around discussing their investments? Or worrying about getting into the university of their choice? Nope. They're having fun.

The word 'romp' is defined in the *Oxford English Dictionary* as 'a spell of rough, energetic play'. When's the last time you went for a romp? The word embodies all kinds of shenanigans, doesn't it? A romp is a bit wild, a bit adventurous, a bit unplanned and always a lot of fun. Your last one was probably a long time ago, unless you're an actual otter or a small child. That's

Otters love a good party. They show up early and leave late and always remember to bring presents.

because romps are impromptu and as adults we're no longer any good at that. We all overschedule ourselves. We drive from A to B with no time for detours. According to a study by professor of psychology and neuroscience Yuko Munakata, this fanatical time management actually makes us less able to take care of ourselves. 'The more time kids had in less structured activities, the more self-directed they were,' says Munakata of the study's results. The reverse was also true: 'The more time they spent in structured activities, the less able they were to use executive function.' It seems clear that in order to live our best lives, we have to plan less. Tell *that* to the next person who asks what you plan on doing with your life.*

> '*My childhood may be over, but that doesn't mean playtime is.*'
>
> *Ron Olson*

---

* This happens a lot when you're an arts or literature student. Take heart that a career in writing about otters is a distinct possibility.

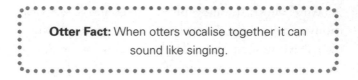

Otter Fact: When otters vocalise together it can sound like singing.

Singing is something we should all do more of – in the car alone, in a choir, with our friends at the club, wherever we can. Not only is it a socially acceptable sort of adult 'play', but the health benefits are numerous. A 2011 study in *Nature Neuroscience* has shown that the act of singing can reduce blood pressure and increase feelings of wellness by releasing dopamine, the feel-good chemical that our brains produce when eating sweets. Singing can also increase cognition and improve posture. Most importantly, perhaps, is that singing in a group has been found to reduce depression and feelings of loneliness in adults. These feelings of wellbeing are thought to be an evolutionary reward of sorts – for being social and cooperating with our fellow humans instead of staying in caves alone. Music psychologist Dr Vicky Williamson, from Goldsmiths College, University of London, told the BBC, 'This paper shows that music is inextricably linked with our deepest reward systems.'

We've all felt this glow of wellbeing. You know that moment when you press play on your favourite song, or one comes on the radio (or is chosen by some streaming-service algorithm), and your brain gets a little excited, and your heart remembers all the good things in the world, and the lyrics all seem to apply directly to your life and experience, and you can't wait to sing the whole thing? And maybe you're on the road, alone, and realise you can sing as loud as you want. Maybe it's 1 am and you're together with friends at the pub, all a little bit sweaty, having fun, and when the song comes on it's a pure belter and you all start belting accordingly, arms around one another, warm with friendship and commonality and joy? *That's* what the otter philosophy is all about. Vocalising pleasure with all your might. Shouting joy out into the universe. Putting that happiness out there for all to see and for everyone to share. And reaping the health benefits in the process. After all, according to singing expert Stacy Horn, author of *Imperfect Harmony: Finding Happiness Singing with Others*, 'Group singing is cheaper than therapy, healthier than drinking, and certainly more fun than working out.' A pretty good endorsement, if you ask me.

Otter-approved Belters
for Furthering Joy

Try reading the following list and not immediately singing aloud to one or more of these classic hits. And keep it handy for your next karaoke session.

- 'Sweet Caroline' by Neil Diamond
- 'Summer of '69' by Bryan Adams
- 'Wannabe' by The Spice Girls
- 'Creep' by TLC
- 'Don't Stop Believin'' by Journey
- 'Livin' on a Prayer' by Bon Jovi
- 'Chasing Cars' by Snow Patrol
- 'Free Fallin'' by Tom Petty
- 'Champagne Supernova' by Oasis
- 'Just a Girl' by No Doubt
- 'Piano Man' by Billy Joel
- 'Big Poppa' by The Notorious B.I.G.

- 'Bohemian Rhapsody' by Queen
- 'We Will Rock You' by Queen
- 'Mr Brightside' by The Killers
- 'Here I Go Again' by Whitesnake
- 'I'm Gonna Be (500 Miles)' by The Proclaimers
- 'Life Is a Highway' by Tom Cochrane
- 'Rolling in the Deep' by Adele
- 'Born to Run' by Bruce Springsteen
- 'I Will Survive' by Gloria Gaynor
- 'I Wanna Dance With Somebody' by Whitney Houston
- 'Flower of Scotland' by Roy Williamson★

★ Unless you're Scottish, you may not be familiar with this one. But trust me when I say there's nothing better than being in a stadium or public square with hundreds or thousands of Scottish people singing this unofficial national anthem together.

If you need me I'll be under these twigs,
dreaming of starfish.

Home and the Environment

'There is nothing like staying at home
for real comfort.'

Jane Austen

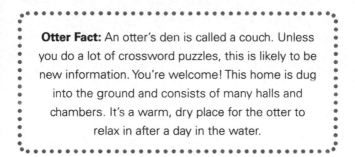

Otter Fact: An otter's den is called a couch. Unless you do a lot of crossword puzzles, this is likely to be new information. You're welcome! This home is dug into the ground and consists of many halls and chambers. It's a warm, dry place for the otter to relax in after a day in the water.

We've been conditioned to believe that our homes should be perfect showcases for our good taste, cleanliness and minimalist tendencies. We're encouraged to curate these spaces with beautiful objects (looking at you, crystals), and to light white sage to purify the air. And then photograph it all, of course! The otter philosophy is less grand. It's about making a warm, dry little space, just for you, where you can relax. Like your couch. Or a basement or den. Or your bed. It doesn't have to be fancy. It doesn't have to have expensive *faux*-fur throws or trendy wallpaper or state-of-the-art electronics (although those are all fine). You don't need a lot of space to relax and be yourself, but you do need a space. Remember those perfectly suitable little hideaways you had as a kid – under a table or at the bottom of a wardrobe or at the top of the house in a secret attic? That's all your soul really needs. Oh, and perhaps just a few cushions, a warm blanket, a cup of tea and a book or two. And a sign that says 'KEEP OUT'.

Unless you're here to play. In which case,
please come in.

Quiz

Where's Your Perfect Otter Home?

Take this quiz to find out where exactly you're meant to live (or vacation), based on those otter nesting instincts of yours.

Your personal decorating style is:

A. lots of handmade textiles, some driftwood and a sheepskin rug

B. white leather couch and tiled floors

C. sculptures by local indigenous artists, pictures of boats

D. ironic communist posters and fresh flowers.

Your ideal Saturday night is:

A. drinks round the pub, some live fiddle music and a lamb curry

B. a nightclub, a few vodkas and see what happens

C. line-caught salmon and organic kale from the local farmers' market, then a long walk

D. cocktails with handmade herbal bitters followed by some Vivaldi at a local arts space.

When it comes to personal style you can usually be found rocking:

A. a Barbour jacket, just like the Queen

B. flannel and Doc Martens

C. a beach cover-up and Gucci flip-flops

D. a flowy skirt and a leather jacket.

If you and your best mate were animals, you'd be:

A. a small pony and a puffin

B. a lizard and a rooster

C. a whale and a crow

D. a swan and a lion.

Answers

Mostly As: a croft on the Shetland Islands. You're a non-conformist otter, happy to be wild and free and far from the madding crowd. Don't let the remoteness fool you, though. The islands are populated with artists, music, good food and a sense of community. Oh, and water. Lots of water.

Mostly Bs: a condo overlooking the beach in the Algarve. White wine, loud music and loads of sunbathing. It's fun, it's carefree – and what's more joyful than a day on the beach with friends? That's the perfect otter life for you.

Mostly Cs: a houseboat in Seattle. You're a real West Coast otter. Close to city life and everything fun that entails, but still a little bit removed from it all. Plus, you love that houseboats are a bit of a laugh. It's a house on a boat!

Mostly Ds: you're a classic river otter. You love a life of culture, yet still want to stick close to nature – the best of both worlds.

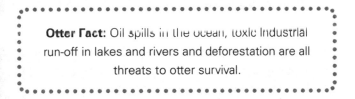

Otter Fact: Oil spills in the ocean, toxic industrial run-off in lakes and rivers and deforestation are all threats to otter survival.

Otters are endangered by the same things we are: human nonsense; greed; environmental deregulation; CO2 emissions. These are serious, life-threatening issues. Climate change is already altering how we live and experience the seasons. The planet is one degree warmer. Our food supply is vulnerable. Access to clean water is under threat. Tropical diseases are making their way north. Movements like Extinction Rebellion are organising against our own annihilation. In the midst of all this it can seem a bit incongruous that we still need to buy milk and loo roll. But, loo roll we must have.

Otters probably also have a sense of when things aren't going well – they were nearly hunted to extinction, after all; surely they must have wondered where all their friends had gone? And yet, while facing despair, they got on with it. Just as life as we know it, today, goes on. Climate change isn't an excuse to skip the homework or stay in bed, although it may seem reasonable, some days. The otter view is about acknowledging the way things are – accepting our grief, anger and then setting them aside, and finding reasons to be joyful, regardless. Ladybirds and quiet human babies are still adorable. Live concerts and driving down a remote highway on a warm night with the windows open is still a rush. Rose gardens and record stores still inspire contemplation. First dates and weddings are still hopeful. The otter view is about minimising daily despair as best you can, and allowing yourself to feel joy in spite of it all. Your mental health is worth it.

Otter Fact: Otters do their part to fight climate change. They don't do it consciously, obviously. They aren't bagging up and recycling all the floating plastic destroying our oceans (looking at you, single-use straws and plastic bags), but they do eat a lot of sea urchins. Sea urchins eat kelp. And kelp eats carbon dioxide. So the more sea urchins the otters eat, the more kelp exists to absorb CO_2 from the atmosphere. Imagine that.

Climate change is an overwhelming thing to think about, as we explored earlier. Unless the entire air travel industry shuts down, the oil companies stop drilling and the politicians agree to a new green deal, switching to energy-saving light bulbs can feel like a bit of a joke. But the point is everyone does their own little bit. And when enough people do their own little bit, it makes a bit of a difference. According to the US Department of Energy, for example, switching the country to exclusively LED lights over the next two decades could reduce electricity consumption from lighting by up to 50 per cent, and avoid 1,800 million tonnes of carbon emissions. And that hopefully makes you feel better about yourself and the world – to know that we're all in this together, everyone bringing their own reusable shopping bags, taking public transportation, recycling, composting, turning off the lights, reducing their dependence on single-use plastics. Doing your part at home and while you're out and about in the world is all part of the social contract. That's why we don't litter. And that's the way the otters would want it.

Otter Fact: Every otter stores a favourite rock in its little chest pouch. The rock is the otter's preferred shape and size for bashing open shellfish, so it makes sense that the otter wants to keep it close.

Having a special place to put our cherished things can be a great exercise in honouring what's important to us. Because we don't have pouches, these special spots can take the form of bookshelves, windowsills, closets, pockets and other various nooks. Some people refer to these special spaces as 'altars' – especially if they're religious or a bit into New Age and spirituality stuff. Traditionally, altars are where sacrifices or rituals take place, so items placed on one can be seen as offerings. To whom? That's up to you. Whatever you call it, making physical space for the things that matter to you – whether they're important tools or things with sentimental value – is one way to practise the otter philosophy.

Creating a space is easy: it can be as simple as a side table with framed pictures of a loved one; a clutch of dried roses from a long-lost love on a bookshelf; a few jagged rocks sparkly with minerals on a windowsill. An altar could even be the front of a refrigerator, covered with drawings by children who love you. Or it can take the form of a perfectly organised wall of tools in the garage. Artists sometimes create altars as an exercise in creativity, adding colourful flowers, bits and bobs from around the house and meaningful photos or text. Perhaps your special items aren't on display, though. Perhaps your special place is private: a metal box or photo album. Maybe your drawer of delicates serves as your spot for safekeeping. Regardless of where you keep them, these special items serve as daily reminders of what's important to you and can help you remember loved ones, inspire nostalgia and delight or give you time for reflection. Honouring these items, and the memories they evoke, is just the otter way.

'Someday you will be old enough to start reading fairy tales again.'

C. S. Lewis, author

'Did you read this, Maxwell? Otters are
very playful animals.'

The Otter Philosophy Reading List

This isn't a list of books featuring otters, but rather books that embody aspects of the otter philosophy. Freedom, joy, adventure, wonder, a sense of humour – you'll find it all in the pages of these otter-approved reads. So curl up on your couch, order in some sushi and settle in for some quirky, joyful stories about life, love, heartache and a few other silly things.

1,047 Reasons to Smile: Little Things that Bring Joy, Happiness, and Excitement by Elizabeth Dutton
This exuberant, funny and very random collection of things to be happy about will definitely make you smile.

The Summer Book by Tove Jansson

In this beloved novel, a little girl lives with joy and abandon on a green Finnish island with her grandmother. She learns about love, nature and even about cats.

And the Birds Rained Down by Jocelyne Saucier

In this remarkable novel, two old friends decide to live out their days on a lake in the forests of Quebec – away from society and immersed in nature. It's all about living your best life, finding love and companionship with your very best friend and ageing gracefully and with joy.

A Year by the Sea by Joan Anderson

During a rocky bit in her marriage, a woman moves to a cottage by the sea in order to recover her sense of self. She spends her days swimming, relaxing on the beach, eating seafood and making new friends. Has a more otter-like book existed?

The Phantom Tollbooth by Norton Juster

Wordplay, puns, a Kingdom of Wisdom and talking animals – this novel is a childhood rite of passage for many book lovers. Read it again, or read it for the first time, and delight in how silly and wonderful the world can be.

The Secret Garden by Frances Hodgson Burnett

What's more joyful and delight-inducing than discovering a secret garden in the grounds of an imposing English estate that you've been sent to live on after your parents die? We can all relate, I'm sure. After our heroine's lonely start, she discovers a magical secret place, and a bunch of friends to enjoy it with.

Kitchen Confidential by Anthony Bourdain

The late Bourdain embodied so many aspects of the otter philosophy: a sense of adventure, a love of food, a willingness to work and a curiosity about pretty much everything. His memoir will inspire you to laugh and probably plan a last-minute trip to New York City.

The Guest Cat by Takashi Hiraide

This international bestseller by a renowned Japanese poet is all about Chibi, a stray cat who adopts a couple living in a guest house in Tokyo. The warm friendship changes everyone for the better – life begins to have more meaning for the couple, the world seems a little bit brighter and the cat gets fed. It's a joyful look at the nature of pet 'ownership' and what it means to love something wild.

The Perks of Being a Wallflower by Stephen Chbosky

This American classic is about living your best, most authentic life, finding humour in the mundane and navigating the often difficult world of being a teenager. It's about embracing the feeling of being young, falling in love for the first time, discovering music and coming to terms with who and what you really are.

The Guernsey Literary and Potato Peel Pie Society by Mary Ann Shaffer and Annie Barrows

This is a very sweet, uplifting novel about a group of English friends who are brought closer by the difficult circumstances of WWII. While living under German occupation on the island of Guernsey, these resilient villagers find joy, humour and even love amid the uncertainty of war. As a bonus, the book takes the form of a series of letters. Letter writing seems like something whimsical that otters would approve of.

'I woke up like this.'

> **Otter Fact.** Otters have the thickest fur of any mammal, with around 850,000 to 1 million hairs per square inch. The two-layered fur system traps air to keep the otter buoyant and prevents their skin from getting wet.

Buoyancy and protection are two of the benefits of having a thick coat. Without a protective layer, people can suffer, too. If we absorb too much of the bad stuff, we sink. (That's what happens to a bald otter.) It's tough out there these days and it's important to insulate your-self from the worst of it – the difficult headlines, the toxic people, the smog, whatever it is that gets you down. That's where the otter philosophy of self-care comes in.

Making time for ourselves, whether to recover, regroup, detox, retox, or whatever it is that makes us feel better, is essential to our survival. Self-care means allowing ourselves to don a little fur coat,* knowing

---

* This is a figurative coat, you understand. Do they even sell new fur coats anymore?

that wearing it protects us from the elements, if only for a little bit. It doesn't mean we can't handle life's hard knocks. Needing a bath or biscuit or a day off on the sofa is not a sign that we're overly sensitive or too precious or in need of a mollycoddle (although there's nothing wrong with any of those things). It's just a sign that perhaps all the nonsense has built up to the point where we need a bit of time to ourselves, safe and warm and away from the elements. To read or window shop or visit a friend or pet a strange dog.

Work and School

'You've achieved success in your field when you don't know whether what you're doing is work or play.'

Warren Beatty

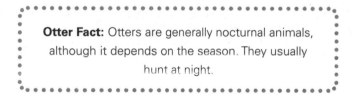

Otter Fact: Otters are generally nocturnal animals, although it depends on the season. They usually hunt at night.

Every few months, it seems, a study is released promoting the health benefits of waking up early: witness all these millionaires who wake up at 4 am and drink cucumber water before their three-hour

Pilates session! The rest of us poor schmucks with no willpower and an urge to sleep in due to severe hangovers will never be as successful as these early birds, the articles imply. But the otter philosophy is about recognising that we're all productive and awake and energetic at different times. In fact, science supports this. A 2019 study at the University of Birmingham's Centre for Human Brain Health found the brainwaves of early birds and night owls are completely different: early birds performed tasks better in the morning, and night owls performed best around 8 pm. So don't fight nature. Some of us are morning people. Some of us need a nap in the afternoon, and some of us are night owls. Or night otters. Awake and getting things done when the rest of the world appears to be sleeping. Cleaning out our cupboards, eating ice cream, writing letters. And this is just fine. There's no best practice when it comes to sleep. You're either getting enough for your own needs or you're not. Whether you're heading to bed at 2 am or 9 pm is not relevant. Night otters of the world, unite!

Otter Fact: It appears that generally, otters as a species have got a bit smaller over time. According to fossils discovered in China's Yunnan province, some prehistoric types of otter used to be the size of wolves. But they're no longer an animal to be reckoned with or feared.

Being ok with being a bit lesser than you'd like, or planned, or were once upon a time, is a good way to come to terms with wherever you're at in life. You may have been a big deal in your high-school maths class, but now you're struggling with your first-year course on black-hole stardust molecules.* Maybe you had a fancy job, but you quit or were fired. Or a fancy partner, but things didn't work out so well. Maybe you inhabited a healthy, fit body and now you're dealing with an illness. Maybe things have changed. You've had a setback. You're not where you

---

*   Or whatever maths classes are called these days. I was an English major.

Just an otter day at the office.

want to be at the moment. You feel you deserve more …

We exist in a world where it's very easy to compare ourselves to those seemingly bigger and better than us and make these feelings of inadequacy worse. It's easy to wallow in despair over what we no longer have. It feels as if we've taken a step back. Take comfort in the fact that it's all part of our personal evolution. No one looks at an otter today and thinks, 'Poor thing. Its ancestors were so much more impressive.' No, we look at an otter enjoying life, surrounded by accepting friends and relishing the sunshine, and think, 'Man, that otter looks content. I wish I knew its secret.'

So, in a world that rewards bigness, be satisfied with the knowledge that personal growth doesn't always mean bigger, bolder, better. And be ok with the knowledge that you're just the right size, at least for now.

'It is utterly false and cruelly arbitrary to put all the play and learning into childhood, all the work into middle age and all the regrets into old age.'

Margaret Mead, anthropologist

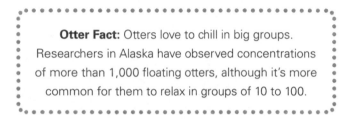

Otter Fact: Otters love to chill in big groups. Researchers in Alaska have observed concentrations of more than 1,000 floating otters, although it's more common for them to relax in groups of 10 to 100.

In an age where independence and individuality are paramount, otters are a great reminder that we can't actually go it alone. Our family, friends, acquaintances and colleagues are all an important part of keeping us afloat. In work parlance, this large, extended group of people is a 'network'. The otter philosophy encourages all sorts of networking – whether it's joining a book club or getting involved at the local hospice, it's all about connecting. This is why we join fraternities,

The otter's commute is always stress-free.

professional societies, arts organisations, sports teams, unions, social networks and political groups. We join because of the opportunities they offer for both personal and professional growth. And the more stuff we do, the more networks we build, whether we realise it or not.

In their book *Connected: The Surprising Power of Our Social Networks and How They Shape Our Lives – How Your Friends' Friends' Friends Affect Everything You Feel, Think, and Do*, scientists Nicholas Christakis and James Fowler found that while most of us only have about three to eight close friends, and about 100 people we may interact with on a regular basis, our networks actually extend much further than that – our communities include friends of friends and even *their* friends and colleagues.* These vast extended networks are often invisible until we least expect it,

---

*   Look no further than social media to understand this fact. How else would you be aware that your aunt's co-worker's daughter just had her fifth birthday (Tinkerbell-themed)? Or that your ex's best friend has a new girlfriend from Cornwall?

but sometimes come to our rescue in a time of need. After all, you never know when someone from your alma mater is going to be interviewing you for a job, when your Spanish teacher's partner might recommend you for an arts grant or when your father's new neighbour might recommend a good lawyer or hiking boot that will change your life. These may seem like very specific examples, but they all happened to someone or other. Probably.

Plus, a strong network is good for your health. The authors of a 2010 study entitled 'Social Relationships and Mortality Risk: A Meta-analytic Review' write: 'The quality and quantity of individuals' social relationships has been linked not only to mental health, but also to both morbidity and mortality.' Accordingly, they found that a stronger social network meant a 50 per cent increase in the likelihood of survival when compared to groups with weaker relationships.

> **Otter Fact:** Otters are part of the weasel (or *Mustelidae*) family that includes skunks, stoats, ferrets, wolverines and badgers. Otters are the only swimmers in the weasel family, however.

We all know people who are so different from their families it's hard to believe they're related. Your buddy has parents in accounting and a sister in finance, while he lives in a caravan, making music at the local arts collective. Or perhaps you've got a friend whose family members are all nuts for the local rugby league, while she's a lover of non-violence and intact brain matter. Perhaps this describes yourself a little bit. Someone who never quite fits in. A vegan in a world of meat lovers. A reader in a world of TV watchers. A substance-loving free spirit in a world of teetotallers. The otter philosophy is about celebrating those differences, embracing what you're good at and forgetting the rest. Imagine if otters looked around and worried that none of their other relatives were swimming. Uncle Skunk and Cousin Ferret think it's weird. But so what? Otters get on with it. They're good at it. It's what they do.

Conversely, sometimes we're bad at things – but discovering this, whether by taking classes at school or trying out a bunch of part-time jobs, is part of our journey on the way to figuring out what we're good at. Once I worked in a receptionist's office filing papers. Because I was a bit of an idiot, I didn't realise that alphabetising involved sorting by more than one letter. So anything beginning with 'R' went somewhere in the 'R' folder – regardless of whether the patient's name was Randall, Rupert or Rza. Luckily, I only worked there a day before being fired, so the chaos I created wasn't too big a deal. But the lesson I learned is that I'm not an organised person and that's just fine. (I also probably don't have a lot of common sense.) My father, however, has alphabetised files of every electronics manual from every record player, phone, dishwasher or computer he's bought since the 1960s. We have different talents, he and I, despite the close relationship. And you've got talents, too. Once you know what those are, the sky's the limit. As the business author Tom

Rath writes: 'You can be a lot more of who you already are.'

Otter Fact: Clean fun keeps the otter afloat. If it gets too dirty, it can drown. Accordingly, otters groom their fur to ensure their survival. If you visit a zoo and the otters are just sitting around licking themselves, tough luck. They're still more entertaining than the sloths, who literally nap for 500 hours at a time.*

Otters do just enough to keep themselves afloat – and no more than that. They aren't spending extra time grooming because someone might be impressed by all that hard work. 'Let me lick this spot for five more hours in case these zoo visitors are amazed by my diligence,' they're likely not thinking. We can learn a lot from this attitude of 'just enough' – those of us

---

* More like 12–15 hours a day, if we're very concerned with the real facts here.

who are overworked, addicted to work or who just can't seem to log off and clock out at a reasonable time. The otter knows we only live once, and the time we have on this planet is limited. Why spend it doing work that's not essential?

Yet, we do. We check our work emails on vacation, we stay late at work without being paid overtime and we generally accept that we need to be available 24/7 to our employers. We have an 'overwork' problem. In fact, in Japan there is even a word for those who die from overwork: *karoshi*. In the UK, employees endure one of the longest work weeks in Europe, but the country has one of the lowest levels of productivity – which means all that extra work isn't worth all that much. A 2014 study by Stanford University found that after about 50 hours a week, we're no longer that productive. After 55 hours, we're basically useless and 70 hours, well, we're pretty much work zombies producing nothing but feelings of sadness and probably a lot of typos. While some companies in places like South Korea, Italy and France are introducing 'Right to Disconnect' legislation, designed to protect citizens from overwork (some companies in Germany actually prevent emails from being delivered to employees' inboxes outside work hours), the rest of us are going to have to go it alone and make sure that we're working to live, and not the other way around. Benefits from setting boundaries between work and play are numerous: reduced stress, an ability to recharge, better sleep, better concentration and, of course, our loved ones will appreciate it, too.

'The best possible preparation for the future is a well-lived present.'

George H. Brimhall, educator

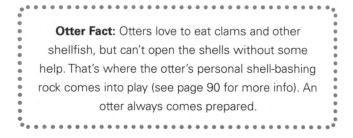

Otter Fact: Otters love to eat clams and other shellfish, but can't open the shells without some help. That's where the otter's personal shell-bashing rock comes into play (see page 90 for more info). An otter always comes prepared.

To an observer, the otter's life appears to be pretty easy. And the secret to that is being a little bit prepared. Not over-prepared, mind you. The otter philosophy isn't interested in life hacks to make you more productive or secret tips for better scheduling. It doesn't encourage keeping a day planner or micro-managing every moment. Stressing out about the future isn't the otter way. Rather, it encourages a bit of preparation, just enough to get by, while acknowl-edging that a little bit of uncertainty is also kind of exhilarating. Ideally, try to prepare just enough to ensure you can enjoy life (and your dinner) without worrying about every possible outcome (that you may or may not have prepared for).

You remember those kids in school who always had 30 different kinds of highlighter? Who studied all night for tests and worried about getting into univer-sity? Perhaps that sounds familiar. After all, we're encouraged from an early age to be prepared for anything. Bring an umbrella – it might rain! But always being prepared can turn into over-preparation, which can be stressful and exhausting – it often means living in the future rather than the present. We have a

Plunging head first into life. While also wearing
sensible swim goggles. Otters are always a bit
prepared for the possibility of fun.

lot to learn from the otter philosophy of not overdoing it. The kids at school who never had a pencil and who always seemed to forget about that day's test? Well, those go-with-the-flow kids all survived, didn't they? They all graduated, became adults and somehow managed to get jobs. And they probably live with a lot less stress, too.

So figure out what your rock is – the essential thing you need to feel prepared at school and work – and try and have it ready when you need it. Maybe it's a spare charger for your phone. Maybe it's lavender oil or your meds. Maybe it's your laptop or plasters for those un-sensible-shoe days. A teeny, weeny bit of preparation can go a long way to making your day a bit easier. But a lot of preparation is often a waste of time, and frankly, it can cramp your style, make you less open to impulsiveness and less likely to plunge in when the opportunity arises. Just like Napoleon said: 'Over-preparation is the foe of inspiration.'

Health and Happiness

'Creative people are curious, flexible, persistent and independent with a tremendous spirit of adventure and a love of play.'

Henri Matisse

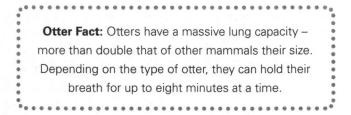

Otter Fact: Otters have a massive lung capacity – more than double that of other mammals their size. Depending on the type of otter, they can hold their breath for up to eight minutes at a time.

Take a big breath. Right now. A big, deep one that gets air into the tips of your toes and the top of your head. Now exhale. Good. Do it again: inhale. Exhale. Life suddenly feels a teeny bit more manageable, right? We know deep breathing is good for us – thanks to the 40 million studies proving that yoga and meditation and deep breathing are stress relieving. Stress causes the shoulders to hunch up, the breath to become shallow – everything tightens. Deep breathing releases that. It helps to activate our relaxation response. Deep breathing strengthens the immune system, it helps improve posture and releases tension. With all that lung capacity and deep breathing, it's no wonder that otters are the least stressed animals on the planet (probably).

'If you retain nothing else, always
remember the most important Rule of
Beauty, which is: 'Who cares?'

Tina Fey

> **Otter Fact:** Sea otters spend a tonne of time grooming themselves. On an average day they can spend up to five or six hours ensuring their fur is clean and tidy. (The rest of the day is spent feeding, sleeping or playing.) They do it because it's necessary for their survival – clean fur keeps them buoyant and dry in the water. It's the exact right amount of grooming, enabling them to keep afloat day after day, and so they do it.

Society loves policing the amount of time we spend on our looks. Too much and we're vain and shallow. *'What is the world coming to?'* Not enough and we don't respect ourselves. *'I remember when people used to put effort into how they looked.'* There are those of us who spend hours watching videos explaining how to contour and how to find the right angles for the best selfie. There are also those of us who like lip balm and rarely look in the mirror. Those of us who wax our bits and those who don't. Those who own brow gel and those who don't. The otter philosophy is about

'It's called a comb-over. They're all the rage.'

finding joy in our daily routines, and not paying attention to the headlines warning that we're becoming more vain than ever before (or that we're abandoning gender norms by not paying close enough attention to our looks).

The thing about what society thinks is that you're never quite exactly right, no matter how hard you try. So embrace whatever it is you do for however long you do it! And don't worry about the otters.

Otter Fact: Every otter has a baggy little chest pouch that's used for storing food. (This is also where the otter keeps its special rock.) It's not particularly noticeable, this pouch, it's just part of the otter's design.

Otters have loose pouches of skin by design – and so do we. They're called 'ageing' and are coming for all of us. Even the Botoxed and the workout buffs and the beautiful teenagers and the scientists searching for the fountain of youth. There's nothing wrong with being a buff hardbody, but neither is there anything wrong with a bit of natural bag and sag. Get used to it! We're all getting older. You're older now than you were when you started reading this sentence. And that means your body has gone a little bit more downhill than it was just moments ago. It's glorious, right? The otter philosophy is all about embracing the realisation that we're all being carried along together in this river of life, morphing, developing, growing, ageing, giving birth, having surgeries, getting sick and getting better, gaining weight and losing it and constantly evolving into newer bodies that are a bit different from the ones we had before. So whether it's a floppy bit of post-birth tummy, a cankle or a turkey-wing arm or a bit of a neck droop, rejoice in the fact that we're all part of nature, and nature loves a good bit of loose skin.* If you can fit little bits of food and tools in yours, so much the better (looking at you, cleavage).

★ See also elephants, Shar Peis and turtles.

Otter Fact: The CIA once designed an otter harness. For unspecified reasons (most *likely* to train otters to deliver explosives or microphones to sensitive locations), the CIA studied otters as part of its infamous MK Ultra project in the 1960s. The organisation's work with otters is outlined in the aptly named 'A Dossier on *Lutra* (The Otter)'.

The otter harness is a great example of a giant institution trying to mould wild minds into something productive at the expense of all else.* We all feel this pressure to conform – at work, at school, on social media. We're all born a bit weird and wild and we're told we need to adapt – squeeze into these societal

---

* At the very least the otter's CIA handlers recognised how adorable and social these creatures were. 'Never, if possible, confine (or leave in zoo or kennel) an otter which has enjoyed any human companionship or freedom,' the report advises. Thanks, Uncle Sam! Perhaps they'll apply this consideration to humans next.

harnesses that have been designed for us. Studies have shown that kids as young as four will adapt their behaviour in order to fit in. Part of the reason for this is self-preservation. We want to graduate, get the promotion, have successful relationships, avoid being the target of online outrage. So the otter philosophy is about recognising when these restraints are useful (schools help us learn, following rules helps us stay out of trouble, paying taxes keeps us out of prison) and when we need to break free and rejoice in our own slippery, joyful freedom. 'Animal resents restricted quarters and will fight and tear itself to destruction to escape,' wrote one official in the otter dossier. Sound familiar? So, if you're feeling trapped or stuck, ask yourself: 'Are these rules/restrictions/societal norms in my best interests? Am I better serving humanity by adapting to these expectations? Or am I delivering payloads of explosives to communist targets on behalf of the US government?' You get the idea. Break free, wild things, whenever it suits you.

> **Otter Fact:** Male otters have a penis bone, or baculum. This bone is often fractured during fights with other animals.

There isn't really a lot to learn from this one except, take care of yourselves, lads. Aggression leads to nothing but trouble, and a trip to A&E.

> **Otter Fact:** While otters embrace the use of tools, they've yet to develop a dependence on technology. It's true. Have you ever seen an otter with a phone?

Not to be too alarmist, but every website and app we interact with is exerting a bit of mind control on us. We're inside that little simulated world, navigating around, scrolling, clicking and behaving like mice in a maze: we learn (scroll here, click here), we're rewarded (notifications, badges) and we come back for more (delicious cheese). We may be there by choice – needing a new pair of shoes or wanting to check up on our friends – but once we're there, we're being forced to navigate inside a bit of software that's designed to influence our behaviours and to keep us coming back again and again. According to a study by UK research firm Ofcom, we check our mobiles on average every 12 minutes, which adds up to about 2.5 hours of phone use a day. That's a lot of hours looking at a tiny screen, no? Consider yourself programmed.

This isn't to say we need to go back to the Stone Age, carrying around flip phones to get the job done. But remember that technology is a tool that serves us, and not the other way around. Or just swap your smartphone for a rock, otter style.

Otter Fact: Otters like to chase their own tails.

There's such a focus in today's busy world on measuring progress, getting ahead, leaning in and learning from mistakes that there's little room for those of us who sometimes go in circles. 'Going in circles', whether it's in a career or in a relationship, is society's code for 'going nowhere'. But the otter philosophy is about acknowledging that there's a time for everything, and it's all part of a process. Some days, weeks or, let's face it, years, can feel as though we're stuck in one place. But there's a lot to be learned from these tail-chasing times in our lives. In fact, contrary to public expectation, we might actually be having fun, something that's hard for those sprinting in one direction to understand. We may know, long term, that a situation isn't good for us. We may not be in line for a promotion, but love the job. We may know that a relationship can't possibly last, but it's a lot of fun. We're not advancing and we're not learning from our mistakes, society tells us. But for now, the situation suits us, and eventually we'll straighten out and get on a path that takes us somewhere else. Or maybe not. What's the rush? There are a lot of reasons for not feeling we're being our absolute best, most productive

Happy to drift along here with my wee pal.
No direction necessary.

selves. The otter philosophy is about knowing that sometimes that happens, and that it doesn't really matter much. At the end of the day, we all end up in the same place (in bed, watching otter videos on our phones).

Otter Fact: Otter cafés are thriving in places like Tokyo and other big cities in Southeast Asia. Patrons pay for the privilege of petting and taking pictures of the resident otters (similar to cat cafés). Some species of otter, however, are listed as vulnerable on the International Union for Conservation of Nature Red List, which means there is debate over the morality of keeping these animals captive for our entertainment.

Travel is all about new experiences … and, these days, it's about documenting those experiences for the folks back home. In fact, too many of us are intent on documenting and posting about every aspect of our lives – especially when we travel. Capturing, containing, manufacturing moments to be shared at the expense of … what? In this case, at the expense of the little otters that are probably a bit miserable, far from their homes and families.

Forty per cent of men surveyed, and 20 per cent of women, admitted that they would even go as far as to post fake holiday photos to social media. Katherine Ormerod, author of *Why Social Media Is Ruining Your Life*, told *CN Traveller*, 'You're creating an idea of a place rather than giving a true reflection of it, and then someone goes and recreates that, and then someone goes and recreates that; it cheapens the process and dilutes the experience.'

But it isn't just animals that lose out when we insist on turning our experiences into content. We lose something fleeting, something essential about ourselves when we see experiences through a social-media lens. We're creating a virtual self that we think others want to see, rather than doing the work to become something different, something weirder or more authentic. Psychotherapist Nancy Colier notes in *Psychology Today* that, 'Instead of being part of it, in the flow of life, we feel as if we have to keep generating new life material, more life stuff, which will announce us, establish us, and ultimately, prove our existence. In the meanwhile, the chasm between us and life grows wider and wider.' The otter philosophy is about doing things because they bring you joy – not likes or followers. It's about experiencing life. Experiencing an exact moment in time. It's about being alive and feeling something – that universal flow – regardless of whether or not it would make a lovely social-media post.

So next time the urge arises to document, post and monitor a response, simply resist. Rather than trapping the moment, let it be free. Let it swirl around in your consciousness. Ruminate on it. Then, if you must, you can always write a poem about how the moment made you feel. That's how we shared our experiences back before the internet:

Gap-year Thoughts
Captive otter
Poses
With roses

snap

Life is hard
Unfair

At least it's not a bear.

Etc.

You remember these. You get the idea.

*'Cheerfulness is the best promoter of
health, and is as friendly to the mind
as to the body.'*

Joseph Addison, English author

Otter Fact: Otters were hunted to near extinction in the 1800s. Their warm pelts were in high demand from the luxury-loving aristocracy in places like England, China and Russia. Eventually, just about a dozen otter colonies of fewer than 100 animals each remained along the west coast of North America. Luckily for the otters, the 1911 International Fur Seal Treaty banned the sale of otter fur, and these small populations bounced back to the healthier levels we see today.

Otters are resilient animals. After facing near extinction, they're now flourishing in our rivers, waterways and oceans. Resilience is an important trait for us to cultivate, both in the workplace and in our relationships – and all it requires is being a bit more open and otter-like, according to researchers.

Psychological resilience is characterised by 'flexibility in response to changing situational demands, and the ability to bounce back from negative emotional experiences', according to a 2004 study in

'Who's feeling resilient now, Bertha?'

the *Journal of Personality and Social Psychology*. The researchers found that resilient individuals tended to feel positive emotions even during a stressful event, helping them to rebound more quickly from the bad experience. And what did all these resilient people have in common? 'They have zestful and energetic approaches to life, and they are curious and open to new experiences,' according to the study's findings. Remind you of anyone? Not only that, but these spirited folks also tend to cope by using humour in times of stress – having a bit of a laugh can raise the spirits of everyone involved. In fact, these people are physically robust as well, displaying a quicker recovery from a cardiovascular event than the less resilient group. It's like when you buy a fancy sausage roll you can't wait to eat and then drop it on the floor – a resilient person might laugh in disbelief, or shrug and pick it up, vowing to eat it anyway. Others might feel distress, embarrassment or sadness for hours over their carelessness.

Not naturally a resilient person? Do you tend to fall down and stay down? Blame yourself? Agonise over something you did or said for days? No problem.

There are a few small ways you can improve this trait, if you're so inclined. It's all about the way you think about things, and psychologist Martin Seligman from the University of Pennsylvania found that there are some cognitive exercises that will help. The first is thinking specifically rather than globally (one issue doesn't necessarily point to a larger problem). The second is acknowledging that external forces are at play, rather than blaming yourself for everything. And the third is recognising that situations are impermanent, rather than permanent. (*'This isn't set in stone; I'll figure out a way to change it.'*) So in short, resilience is about looking at our problems as specific, external and impermanent. Easy, right? If you're an otter.

'I'm just here to party.'

A Note on Endings

WHAT WE CAN LEARN FROM EDDIE THE OTTER

*'… merriment … bars a thousand harms
and lengthens life.'*

William Shakespeare

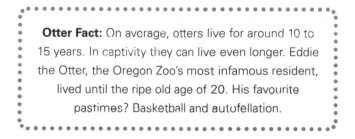

Otter Fact: On average, otters live for around 10 to 15 years. In captivity they can live even longer. Eddie the Otter, the Oregon Zoo's most infamous resident, lived until the ripe old age of 20. His favourite pastimes? Basketball and autofellation.

Eddie was one of the world's most beloved otters when he passed away in 2018. To help the arthritis in his elbows, his minders gave him a basketball hoop to play with, and videos of him dunking have nearly 2 million views. Videos of him engaging in his other favourite pastime are also pretty popular. 'Yes, that was Eddie who displayed so much "confidence" in front of zoo guests,' a zoo spokesperson confirmed after his death.

So what's the otter philosophy of death? Choose a good life. That's pretty much it. There's a reason YOLO is one of the key tenets of the otter philosophy. Live with joy and enthusiasm every day. None of us knows what's in store. No matter how healthy we are now, or how good our genes are, something's going to get us in the end. It may be environmental, it may be genetic, it may be a bus. Whatever it is, the best way to ensure a good death is to live a good life. And not take ourselves too seriously.

May we all live and die like Eddie the Otter: doing what gives us pleasure, other people's expectations be damned.

In Conclusion:
You Otter Know!

Otters remind us of what it's like to feel truly alive. Watching an otter play, twirl, dunk and dive is one of life's simple pleasures. To see an animal so truly in the moment – unafraid of predators, not worried about dinner, not fighting or mating or taking care of pups; just engaged in a game of tag or wrestling – it's easy to see how the chatty little otter and her playmates have inspired a whole philosophy.

So I hope it's clear by now that the otter philosophy and the PLAY method have a lot to offer us joyless, work-obsessed mortals. Perhaps from now on, you'll allow yourself to enjoy a bit more fun. You'll keep an eye out for opportunities to get wet, ask questions, seize the day and lighten up a bit. After all, you made it here. Both to the end of this book and to this moment in time on the planet. You did it!

You're still alive! And what better cause for celebration? You deserve a good laugh. A romp. A singalong. Some loving kindness. Go on, take it. That's it. Now throw it up in the air. Give it a nibble. A little hug. That's it. Because the otternative – a very serious life – is just too bleak to contemplate.

In conclusion, life is very short, enjoy it like you otter.

A Collection of Otter-Approved Things for Future Reference

- Handshakes
- Five-course meals
- Pinky swears
- Slinkies
- Beer with friends
- A picnic
- Tree climbing
- Group texts with exclamation marks
- The big smile emoji
- Karaoke
- Water parks
- Large, soft blankets
- Sushi
- Beauty routines
- Dirt

- Hugs
- Smashing things with rocks*
- Somersaults
- Naps
- Laughter
- Eating with your hands
- Pub trivia

* Not in a serial-killer way. In a fun, outdoorsy adventure way.

One fish, starfish, shellfish, go fish. Otters aren't
concerned about the rules, particularly,
as long as they're having fun.

Acknowledgments

Many thanks to my agent, Euan Thorneycroft, and to my editor, Lydia Good. Thanks to Clare Faulknor for the brilliant illustrations. And many thanks to the wonderful team at HarperCollins – my copy editor, Anne, who turned the Zs into Ss, the proofreaders, production team, marketing, publicity and sales – to every bookseller and librarian who helps to make books like this a success.

HarperCollins*Publishers*
1 London Bridge Street
London SE1 9GF

www.harpercollins.co.uk

First published by HarperCollins*Publishers* 2019

1 3 5 7 9 10 8 6 4 2

Text and poetry © Jennifer McCartney 2019
Illustrations © Clare Faulkner 2019
All poetry is the author's own unless otherwise stated

Jennifer McCartney asserts the moral right to
be identified as the author of this work

A catalogue record of this book is
available from the British Library

HB ISBN 978-0-00-834796-3
EB ISBN 978-0-00-834182-4

Printed and bound in Great Britain by
CPI Group (UK) Ltd, Croydon, CR0 4YY

MIX
Paper from
responsible sources
FSC™ C007454

This book is produced from independently certified FSC™ paper
to ensure responsible forest management.

For more information visit: www.harpercollins.co.uk/green